We All Pull

A Folktale from Russia • Retold by John Porell

There is a big turnip in our garden.
We want the turnip!

My grandfather is strong. He pulls.

My grandmother is tall. She pulls.

My father is strong. He pulls.

My mother is big. She pulls.

My sister is big.
She pulls.

8

10

Look!
We have the turnip!

Facts About Families

What do families do?

read

play

eat

hug

What does your family do?

13

Fun with Families

Match the word to the person.

brother   **father**   **sister**

grandfather   **mother**   **grandmother**

Mark an ✕ by the answer.

1. Which is small?

_____ ✕

2. Which is big?

_____ _____

3. Who is tall?

_____ _____

4. Who is young?

_____ _____

Glossary

garden

pull

strong

turnip